TRANS* ALLY WORKBOOK

Getting Pronouns Right
& What It Teaches Us About Gender

BY DAVEY SHLASKO

Illustrated by KAI HOFIUS

OAKLAND, CALIFORNIA · 2014

TRANS* ALLY WORKBOOK:
Getting Pronouns Right
& What It Teaches Us About Gender

© 2014 DAVEY SHLASKO

ILLUSTRATIONS BY KAI HOFIUS

DESIGNED BY
SOPHIE ARGETSINGER

ISBN 978-0-9906369-0-8
2nd printing August, 2014

Thanks to the many people who provided their personal insights and feedback on this booklet, including:

RACHEL BRIGGS, CHASE CATALANO,

SUMMER CORRIE, CIAN DALZEL, JONAH ALINE DANIEL,

SONNY DUNCAN, ILANA GERJUOY, KATJA

HAHN D'ERRICO, ERIC HAMAKO, SARAH HERSHEY,

KAI HOFIUS, RAMESH KATHNANDA, JOANNA KENT KATZ,

DANE KUTTLER, NELL MYHAND,

LIORA O'DONNELL GOLDENSHER,

MARGARET SHLASKO, & SHANNON WAY

TABLE OF CONTENTS

TABLE OF EXERCISES

S O YOU WANT TO BE AN ALLY to your trans* friends, relatives or coworkers. Great! Thanks for being on board. You know that being an ally is about behavior, not just intention, so you've been doing your homework: You went to a workshop, you learned all about the difference between sex, gender and sexual orientation, and you proudly explain that you believe trans* people should be safe from violence and discrimination. But there's one thing that's still tripping you up …

Pronouns. Why are pronouns so hard? What makes it so easy to slip up and call your trans* friend by a pronoun they don't use anymore—maybe even since before you knew them?

I lost count long ago of the number of times a friend or colleague called me the wrong pronoun even though they knew better, and then when I reminded them they said, "It's hard. We're trying." Their defensive response was inappropriate and difficult for me to hear, because it implied that my transition was harder for them than it was for me, or that the pace of my transition should depend on their comfort. Still, there was some truth in it and eventually I started to believe them: It really is difficult (sometimes), and "trying harder" isn't necessarily effective. Instead of asking them to try harder, I got curious about what exactly was making it difficult—what was in the way of their doing this simple behavior that they obviously wanted to do?

> TRANS* (adj.): Anyone whose *gender identity* and/or *gender expression* differs significantly from what is expected of them in their culture based on their *sex assigned at birth*, including people who are *transgender, transsexual, genderqueer,* and more.

I decided to investigate what exactly makes pronouns so challenging. I interviewed dozens of people about what makes it hard for them, if/when it is hard, to get someone's pronouns right. Based on their responses and my own experiences, I developed exercises to help people get pronouns right, and started using the exercises in some of my trans* inclusion workshops. Over the years, participants talked to me about their challenges and about what helped, and I incorporated their responses into my work with trans* allies. This booklet brings it all together: A compilation of insights, explanations and exercises that can help you figure out what is getting in your way, and to get past it, so that your good intentions can translate into respectful action.

Will getting pronouns right make you the best trans* ally ever? No, not quite. Even though you might need to put significant thought and effort into it at first, it's important to recognize that calling someone the right pronouns is a pretty low bar. The steps you take next will be up to you—you'll find resources at the back of this booklet that can help you think about some possibilities. Meanwhile, by using this booklet as a companion to your trans* ally work, you can make sure that you'll show up as the respectful, committed and caring person you are.

This booklet will be most useful for people who have participated in a trans* inclusion training of some kind, or who at least have some basic familiarity with the vocabulary of trans* issues. If trans* issues are totally new to you, you can still get something from this booklet, but it probably won't be all you need to feel confident in your understanding of what it takes to be a trans* ally. If you are part of a group or organization addressing trans* inclusion and working to become better allies together, consider scheduling a workshop with Think Again Training (more info in the back) that can further illuminate the ideas in this booklet and help you make the most of your learning.

HOW TO USE THIS BOOKLET

In this booklet you'll find some information about trans* identities and experiences, some ideas about how the binary gender system impacts all our thinking and language, and some suggestions of tools and exercises (highlighted in the pink boxes) that may make it easier for you to call people the pronouns they've asked to be called.

Not everyone who accidentally calls someone the wrong pronouns is doing so for the same reasons. Some of the reasons outlined in this booklet might not be true for you, while others might be spot on. It's your job to think about each section and figure out whether the pattern described is one that you fall into.

Likewise, some of the exercises will be exactly what you need, and some won't. If it seems helpful, do it. If not, then it might not be the one for you (at least not right now). Some of the exercises can be done alone, while some require other people's participation. Whether or not you choose to do the exercises, sharing and discussing this booklet with a friend will probably make it even more useful than reading it alone.

Terminology. The language we use to talk about trans* issues is constantly evolving. Brief definitions are provided throughout the booklet for words that may be new to many readers. A more extensive glossary is located in the back. People use these terms in a variety of ways, and their usage has changed and will continue to change over time. When referring to an individual's identity, it's more important to understand what that person means by the terms they use, rather than to memorize the "standard" definitions.

WHAT EXACTLY ARE PRONOUNS?

Grammatically, pronouns are words that we use in place of nouns, to avoid repeating those nouns. In this case, we're talking about the third person singular pronouns: he, him, his, she, her, and hers. In standard English (and many other languages, but not all), third person singular pronouns are always gendered.

Most people like to get called one set of pronouns and not others—for example, he, his and him but not she, hers and her. (This is true of cisgender people as well as trans* people.) Some people don't like to be called either of the two most common sets

> CISGENDER (adj.): Non-trans*.

of pronouns, and instead ask to be called they/their/them as singular pronouns or another set of "gender-neutral" or non-binary pronouns, such as ze/hirs/hir, per/pers, zie/zirs/zir, etc.

In general, people want to be called the pronouns that "go with" their gender identity. However, sometimes a person might need to be called a pronoun that doesn't feel right to them, in order to preserve their safety and/or privacy. Or, a person may ask to be called the pronoun that works best for them in some situations—such as among people who are safe and understanding—but not in other situations—such as in front of their boss if the person is not "out" at work. Like with gender identity, the pronouns someone wants to be called may change one or more times over of the course of their life.

When somebody tells you what pronoun they want to be called, or that

> A NOTE ABOUT PRONOUN "PREFERENCE": You may hear people talk about *"preferred gender pronouns"* (or PGPS). Some trans* people object to this phrase, because the word "preferred" implies that it is only preferable, not mandatory, to call someone by the pronoun they have asked for. In this booklet I have chosen to say "the right pronoun" or "the pronoun someone wants to be called" rather than PGP.

they want to be called a different pronoun than before, they will not necessarily tell you why. The reason may be complex, and besides, you don't really need to know. All you need to know is which pronouns they want you to use when referring to them. If your relationship is very close they may also want to talk with you about their gender journey in more detail, but you can safely expect to have that conversation far less often than the conversation about pronouns.

Some people whose gender identities are outside the binary (not simply a man or a woman, such as genderqueer people), ask to be referred to using "gender-neutral" or non-binary pronouns. Not everyone with a non-binary identity wants to be called non-binary pronouns. You can also use non-binary pronouns to talk about hypothetical individuals or individuals whose gender is unknown (instead of saying something like "he or she"). You'll notice me using they/them/theirs in this way throughout this booklet.

> GENDERQUEER (adj.): One of many identity labels used by trans* people whose gender identity does not fit into either of the two most widely-recognized gender categories (men and women).

Although many people call them "gender-neutral pronouns," I tend to say "non-binary" instead, for several reasons: First, the implications of asking people to call you these pronouns are anything but "neutral." On the contrary, going by non-binary pronouns can make a strong statement about one's personal and/or political relationship to gender. Also, in most other contexts, "gender-neutral" means inclusive of all genders, or not gender-specific. (For example, a gender-neutral restroom is one that anybody can use, regardless of gender.) I prefer not to confuse that definition by also using "gender-neutral" to refer to pronouns that are specifically non-binary.

Some people use non-binary pronouns to refer to everybody, as a way of challenging the binary assumptions in our languages. This is sometimes problematic, because many people (including many trans* people) feel disrespected when they are not called by the gendered pronouns that feel right to them.

WHY IT MATTERS

If you picked up this booklet you probably already agree that it is important to call people the pronouns they ask to be called. Still, it can be useful to remind yourself why.

Most of the time, most people are on autopilot about pronouns. They call all women she, her and hers, and all men he, him and his. But being on autopilot doesn't always work. Sometimes—especially, but not only, when talking about trans* people—it can lead you to call someone a pronoun that isn't what they're usually called or what they want to be called. It may be the most painful thing you could possibly call them.

Why would it be so painful? When you use a gendered pronoun about someone, you are in effect announcing that person's gender. Most people feel attached to their gender as a core aspect of their identity. When you announce it incorrectly, it can imply that you don't recognize or "believe in" the person's gender identity.

Being mis-pronouned can have a particular impact on trans* people because, whereas most cisgender people can comfortably assume that their gender is obvious and legitimate, trans* people's genders are contested. Many trans* people—especially those whose transitions are recent, or who don't "pass" as the gender with which they identify, or who identify outside of the two socially sanctioned gender categories—are accustomed to our genders being questioned, ignored or denied in almost every interaction.

TRANSITION can refer to any of the medical, social, legal, spiritual and personal processes that a trans* person may go through in order to live their life in a way that works for their gender. Asking people to call them a different pronoun than before can be part of someone's transition.

Many trans* people experience physical and emotional violence based on others' denial of or objection to their gender identities. Pronoun slipups, however unintentional, are connected to the broader reality of systemic violence against trans* people, and can function as microaggressions—brief and commonplace interactions that intentionally or unintentionally communicate bias and reinforce a system of oppression.

The specific impact on a trans* person when someone calls them the wrong pronoun varies depending on the context, on the support they have access to, and on their relationship with the person who messed up. Possible impacts include:

+ Annoyance
+ Confusion
+ Feeling unrecognized or invisible
+ Feeling unreal or not really present, distanced or dissociative
+ Triggering internalized oppression, feeling not feminine or masculine "enough"
+ Feeling disrespected
+ Feeing unsafe
+ Being "outed" to observers who weren't aware of their trans* status
+ Losing relationships with observers who weren't aware of their trans* status
+ Being targeted for violence based on their trans* status

In addition to the impact on the person who you mis-pronouned, there's also an impact on you and your ability to show up as your best self. When you're trying hard to get someone's pronouns right and continually making mistakes, you end up putting a lot of energy into pronouns that could be better spent another way. Instead of focusing on what you both value about your relationship, you can get stuck in a frustrating and unproductive cycle of feeling nervous, saying the wrong thing, feeling badly about having said the wrong thing, and saying the wrong thing again.

It's normal to mis-pronoun someone once or twice when they first change their pronoun. The goal of this booklet is to help you learn from your mistakes quickly, so that you can get out of that cycle and move on to the conversation you want to be having, with everyone feeling respected, seen and safe.

There are many ways to answer the question of why it is important to call people the pronouns they want to be called. In some ways the most important reason is *your* reason—why does it matter *to* you? The exercises below can help you clarify and solidify your motivation to do the work you need to do to get pronouns right.

Reflection: Clarifying Motivation

Think of one trans* person for whom you have difficulty using the right pronouns. Who is this person? What is your relationship to this person? In your own words, why is it important for you to get this person's pronoun right? What could be the consequences for you and them of continuing to get the pronoun wrong? Take some time to write down your thoughts about this. Put the paper in a place where you will see it at least once a day. Read it over from time to time. Even if you don't read it every day, simply noticing that it's there can serve as a gentle reminder.

Check In: Commitment

If it feels appropriate, talk to the person about why it's important to you that you get their pronoun right. Saying it aloud to the person who is most affected reinforces your own motivation, and also lets the person know that you are taking this seriously.

Only do this if you two are close, and if you have asked for and received permission to talk with this person about your learning process. You may want support and company in this journey, and that's valid—but seek it out elsewhere, because it is not this person's responsibility. Rather than assuming that they will be available to help you (and everyone else) understand their gender or navigate their transition, take responsibility for doing your own work to be the ally you want to be, and invite this person to participate in your process *if* they choose to.

Barriers to Getting Pronouns Right, and How to Overcome Them

"I'M JUST NOT USED TO IT"

The most obvious reason it may be hard to get someone's pronoun right is simply because it's a change. Whether you've known someone for two weeks or twenty years, if you got used to calling them one pronoun (and/ or name) and now they're using a different one, you might have to work to change the habit. (If you *didn't* know them before, and their pronoun feels like a change from what you'd *expect*, that's a different thing. See below under The Binary Gender System.)

In this situation, you have a unique opportunity to be a really valuable ally by doing what you need to do to get the person's pronouns right. Most trans* people lose at least a few friends during transition. Some of those friends mean well, but get so caught up in their own feelings about the transition that they can't see through them to find ways to support their trans* friend. By calling someone the right pronouns even though it's hard, you can show them that you are one friend who they won't have to lose. You can also demonstrate that the image of them that you have in your head is an image of who they are now, not an image of them in the past or as you wish they would be. By using the right pronouns you can say, "I see you, I recognize you, I accept that you are who you say you are."

If habit is all that's getting in your way, there is good news: it just takes practice. The practice exercises below can help.

While you're finding ways to practice using the right pronouns, don't stop reading—you may find there are other factors getting in your way, in addition to habit.

EXERCISES TO PRACTICE PRONOUNS:

1. *Gossip (not really)*
Talk about the person when the person is not around, using the pronouns the person has asked you to use. You don't have to be talking about the person's gender. Just mention the person in your regular chit chat about your day. If you know the person in

8

a confidential setting, try talking about the person to yourself in private, such as in the shower. Get used to thinking, saying and hearing the person's name paired with the right pronoun.

2. *Toy Story*

Give names to several common household objects in your home. For any object that has gendered associations for you, give it another gendered name. (For example, your mixing bowl might be Jack and your chopping knife might be Dolores.)

While you're going about your daily routine, tell stories about the objects using the pronouns appropriate to their names. Tell the stories aloud. Actually saying and hearing the pronouns is an important part of this learning process.

Once you've got that down (after at least a few days, or however long it takes for the objects' new genders to feel "natural"), switch pronouns but not names. Now the mixing bowl would still be Jack, but her pronoun would be "she." Once that feels natural, switch back. Switch back again. Add additional objects or try using non -binary pronouns to make the game more challenging.

This practice can help to limber up your pronoun-switching muscles. Rather than relying on what "feels right" to you about another person's gender, you're training yourself to use the pronoun you've been told is right for them.

3. Accountability
If it feels appropriate, make a plan with the person about how they can remind you if you mess up. For example, can they interrupt you in the middle of a sentence to correct you? Can they call you the wrong pronoun each time you call them the wrong pronoun? The point is not to be punitive, but to agree on a way that you can get immediate feedback and not slip into old habits, and they can let you know when your incorrect pronoun use impacts them. Like the Commitment exercise above, you should only do this if you are close, and if both people agree to do this process together.

4. Community
Do it together! If someone in your community is transitioning, don't be afraid to connect with other people in your community about what that means to all of you. Talk with other allies who are also trying to be respectful. Agree to remind each other when you slip up, so that it's not always the trans* person's responsibility to do it. Consider getting together to discuss any issues that might get in your way, to go over some of the exercises in this booket, or just to practice.

Calling someone a recently-coined non-binary pronoun (or title, like Mx.—parallel to Ms. or Mr., sounds like mix) can be especially difficult at first, simply because it is a new word. But you can do it! It just takes practice. In addition to the exercises above, try this:

Non-Binary Journaling

If you already keep a journal, continue writing about whatever it is you usually write about, but use non-binary pronouns (whichever set you're trying to learn)—for everybody. If you don't already keep a journal, set aside 15 minutes a day to write about something that happened to you that day, using only non-binary pronouns. You'll be surprised how quickly they flow "naturally" in your writing. Then it just takes a little getting used to, to use them in speech.

CLOSE TO HOME: FOR PARTNERS, FAMILY MEMBERS, AND CLOSE FRIENDS

For the people who are closest to someone who transitions, getting pronouns right can be a particular challenge. If your parent, child, sibling, lover, partner, or best friend since childhood is transitioning and wants to be called a different pronoun, the closeness of your relationship can make their transition feel personal, as though it's about your identity as well as theirs.

In a sense, this is an illusion. It's not about you and there's nothing you can do or could ever have done to make it happen or not happen. In another way, it is about you, because their identities have something to do with your identities. For example, if your child was assigned male at birth, you may be used to thinking of yourself as the parent of a son. Now she's transitioning and wants to be called she. It might be hard for you not only because it's hard to think of her as a woman, but also because it's hard to think of yourself as the parent of a daughter.

If it's your partner who's transitioning, there may be an additional element about sexual orientation. You may be used to thinking of yourself not only as someone who is partnered with someone of a particular gender, but as someone who *would only ever* be partnered with someone of a particular gender. Learning that your partner is transitioning may call into question your understanding of your own sexual orientation.

If any part of this sounds like it reflects something that's going on for you, try the following exercises.

Check In: Relational Identities

Check in with your loved one who's transitioning about relational identity words. For some trans* people, it's true that transitioning means a shift in all the relational identities that might apply to them—wife, brother, father, aunt and so on. For others, it can feel okay or even great to live with the seeming-contradiction of, for example, being a guy who's always called he/him/his and is also someone's sister or daughter or mom. When someone transitions, their relational identities may change a lot, or they may not change at all. Rather than assuming, *ask* what they're thinking about that.

Reflection: Relational Identities

Journal and reflect on your own relational identities—as the father of a son, or as a wife who has a husband, or whatever it is—and on your sexual orientation if relevant (more on that below). Which of your identities feel implicated in the transition? How do you feel about that? What would it mean for you to shift your understanding of those identities? What would it mean for you *not* to shift your understanding of those identities? This is your part of your loved one's transition. You may need space and time to figure out what it means to you. Creating opportunities for your own process will help you be grounded and realistic through the transition process and make you a far stronger ally in the end. In addition to reflecting individually, it can be helpful to talk with other people who have a similar relationship to a loved one who is trans*.

Reflection: Sexual Orientation

Here are some questions to consider if your sexual orientation is in the mix: Does it feel like a *problem* for you to think of yourself as, for example, a lesbian whose partner is now a man, or a straight woman whose partner is genderqueer? Does it feel like a *contradiction* that's *not* a problem? Or does it only *sound like* a contradiction relative to the dominant understandings of sexual orientation, while in fact it makes perfect sense for you? Or what? If it is a contradiction, how would it feel to sit with the contradiction? How would it feel to resolve the contradiction by thinking of your sexual orientation in a different way? You may not have answers immediately—that's okay! It's helpful to ask yourself these questions with open curiosity, rather than assuming that your partner's transition either *must* mean something or *can't* mean anything about your sexual orientation. Your partner's gender is what it is and is not negotiable, but you are the one who gets to decide what it means to you.

THE BINARY GENDER SYSTEM

Have you ever found yourself saying or thinking anything like …

If Ben's voice was lower it would be easier to call Ben "he" instead of "she."

If Jeanne didn't have a 5 o'clock shadow it would be easier to call Jeanne "she" instead of "he."

If Barry didn't have breasts it would be easier to call Barry "he."

If Wanda wasn't so tall it would be easier to call Wanda "she."

If Jae wasn't so pretty and feminine looking, it would be easier to call Jae "they" instead of "she."

The binary gender system refers to the faulty assumption that an individual's sex, gender identity, and gender expression always line up in predictable ways—for example, that everyone who is born with a uterus identifies as a woman and expresses herself through femininity—and further that there are two and only two sexes, and two and only two genders (where identity and expression are conflated). *This is just not true.* At the same time, since most of us are taught to believe in this model, its impact on our lives is very real.

When you find yourself thinking "If only that person's body was more like what I usually think of as a female body, it would be easier to call the person 'she,'" the binary gender system has snuck into your thinking. You're working on an assumption—even though you may not believe it consciously—that all women have bodies like those we usually call 'female,' and all men have bodies like those we usually call 'male'—or should. You're relying on the binary gender system, even though you know it's not an accurate reflection of human diversity. And this is heartbreaking because *the binary gender system assumes and asserts that trans* people don't exist.* It especially asserts that non-binary identified trans* people (those who identify as neither a man nor a woman, or as both, or as something else) don't exist. When you misgender someone based on biology, you imply that trans* people aren't real.

The binary gender system not only makes trans* people invisible, but also ignores the variety of bodies that exist among trans* and cisgender people. It implies that the only way to be a man is to be tall, hairy, and muscular, and the only way to be a woman is to be petite, smooth-skinned, and slender. Often, it relies on specific norms of what it means to be male or female that assume not only gender but also other factors like white racial heritage, average size for men and smaller-than-average size for women, and the absence of disability, illness, and aging—which means that these norms are realistic only for a tiny proportion of the population, for a short period in their lives.

When we think about it, we know that the assumptions of the binary gender system are not true, but we've been taught to believe in them so thoroughly that sometimes they sneak into our thinking anyway. It's important to notice the underlying assumptions that we're acting on, so that we can choose to act, instead, on what we know to be true—that people have all kinds of bodies and all kinds of genders, all equally valid and real.

Sometimes the gender binary sneaks into people's thinking in a way that's not about bodies, but rather about gender roles—about womanly or manly behavior. For example people have confided to me that it's hard for them to call a trans* woman "she" if she walks "like a guy," communicates directly, or shows confidence in her viewpoints. People have told me it's hard to call me "he" because I'm "nice," good with kids, and artistic. In this case, it seems to me that the underlying assumption is not only that body type dictates gender, but also that gender dictates personality. Anyone whose mannerisms don't match the cultural expectations of womanly behavior, for example, doesn't really count as a woman.

It's hard for me to call Alex "he" because he is so nice.

It's hard for me to call Allie "she" because she's so strong and athletic.

It's hard for me to call Lou "they" because they just don't seem genderqueer to me.

It's hard for me to call May "she" because she's so angry.

It's hard for me to call Max "he" because he is so emotional.

I know you don't really believe that men can't be emotional, or that women can't be angry. And by now you know that it doesn't matter how someone's gender seems to you—it matters how it seems to them. Assumptions that link a gender group with a universal human trait, like having feelings, are not only harmful to trans* people; they hurt everyone. They reinforce an expectation that women (including both trans* and cisgender women) must be ladylike and men (including both trans* and cisgender men) must be manly, or face the consequences—such as invisibility, exclusion, and violence. They can put pressure on trans* and cisgender men and women to perform stereotypical versions of masculine or feminine gender expression in order to be accepted as the gender they are. They invisibilize and marginalize genderqueer and other non-binary identified people. These assumptions are incredibly damaging to all of us. Rooting them out of our language and pronoun use goes hand in hand with rooting them out of other aspects of our thinking.

MEDICAL TRANSITION AND THE GENDER BINARY

Assumptions about gender can also sneak into our thinking and behavior in some specific ways related to medical transition. Most straightforwardly, people often find it easier to call someone the right pronouns after they've started to take hormones or after they've had transition-related surgery. This pattern implies an assumption that someone can be a woman if she *had* a male body, but not if she *still has* a body that is like those we usually categorize as male. This is problematic for a bunch of reasons:

+ Trans* people are the genders they say they are, whether or not they choose to change their bodies.

+ The assumption creates external pressure on trans* people to change their bodies whether or not that's what they need for themselves.

+ Medical transition can be costly; many trans* people who want and need to utilize medical transition options are not able to access them.

+ It still buys into the sex/gender binary, by assuming that a man's body means a body that looks like those we usually categorize as male (whether it developed that way with or without medical intervention), and a woman's body means a body that looks like those we usually categorize as female (whether it developed that way with or without medical intervention). That's a tiny step farther than implying that trans* folks don't exist at all, but only a very tiny one.

Some people find it easier to call someone the right pronoun after the person has announced plans to take medical transition steps, even before their bodies start to change. When I decided I was going to start taking testosterone and started telling people that, several colleagues who had struggled with my pronouns suddenly found they were able to call me "he" with no problem. During the six months between deciding to take testosterone and actually getting a prescription, my body didn't change, and my identity didn't change, but people's belief in my gender did.

The underlying assumption that seemed to be playing out wasn't as simple as that I had to have a masculine body to be a guy. It was that I had to have the intention to have a masculine body. To me, this reflects a widely-held—but wrong—belief that trans* people who change their bodies are "really" the genders they say they are, while trans* people who don't or can't change their bodies are not as real or legitimate.

Reflection: The Binary Gender System

If you notice some underlying beliefs poking through in your behavior around pronouns, whether those assumptions are about bodies, gender roles, medical transition or something else, here are some questions to reflect on. Use them as writing prompts for reflective journaling, or as prompts for discussion with someone you trust.

+ Based on the examples above, what are some assumptions about gender that you have found yourself thinking or acting on? (Try to generate a list, not just one example.) How have they come up? How do you feel about that?

+ Other than making it hard to use the right pronouns for a trans* person you know, what else in your life might also be affected by these same assumptions? For example, how might they affect your relationships with people who have the same gender identity as you? What about your relationships across gender? How might it affect your interactions with children? With your students, clients or coworkers? How might it affect how you think about yourself?

+ When you think about it consciously, in what ways do you agree and disagree with these assumptions? What *do* you believe about gender? What would it look like to act on those beliefs?

INTERPERSONAL FACTORS

There are lots of ways that our feelings about someone—whether conscious or unconscious—can come out in our behavior, including in our pronoun use. For example, one time when I had been out as trans* and working in trans* community for about five years, a colleague of mine transitioned and I had the hardest time calling her by her new pronouns. By that point I had known *a lot* of people who had transitioned, and it had never been hard for me before. At first I couldn't understand what made this transition so challenging for me.

I reflected with the help of a trusted friend, and before long I figured out why I was struggling with my colleague's pronouns—I didn't like her. I disagreed with some of how she was doing her job, and we were not getting along. It had nothing to do with her gender, and even if it had, that would obviously not be an okay reason to call her the wrong pronouns.

As soon as I recognized what was going on, it stopped being a barrier to my using the right pronouns, and I was able to call her the pronouns that she wanted easily and consistently. As a result, my attention (and probably hers, too) was freed up to figure out what our conflict was actually about. Had I not tried to figure it out, and instead kept beating myself up every time I got her pronoun wrong, we might never have had that opportunity to address our real disagreements and become better colleagues to each other. Because I figured out what was going on *with me* that made it hard for me to call her the right pronouns, I was able to show up with all the compassion and skill that I usually bring to professional relationships.

It's my belief that you are not obligated to like everybody, but you are obligated to treat everybody with basic respect and dignity, and that includes respecting their gender whether or not you enjoy each other's company. If you have an issue with someone, take the opportunity to figure out what the issue is and decide what to do about it, rather than taking it out on their gender. Here are some more complicated examples of social or interpersonal factors that might get in the way of someone using the right pronouns ...

Being in the Same Club. Sometimes, the pronoun you tend to default to for someone else depends on whether or not you perceive the other person as part of your in-group in terms of gender and/or sexual orientation. One person told me that she has seen many friends transition, and usually finds it easy to switch to calling someone a new pronoun. But she described one time when it was harder. She is a queer and genderqueer woman, and for years her friend also identified that way. Their similarity in terms of gender was part of their relationship. When her friend's gender experience shifted and he started asking people to call him he/him/his, she struggled because she was used to seeing their genders as the same. She thought, "If he's a guy ... what does that mean about me?" Of course, she knew that it didn't need to mean anything about her. But her feeling that her friend was "like her" made it difficult for her to separate his gender from her own.

A similar dynamic can play out if you *don't* see someone as "in the club." If as a cisgender woman you meet a trans* woman who, for whatever reason, you don't want to think of as "one of the girls," it may be harder to respect her gender pronouns than if you felt excited to welcome her into your circle. Sometimes the reason that you don't want to think of a trans* person as part of your gender group might come from the same kind of implicit disbelief in trans* identities that I described above as part of the binary gender system. Other times it might be about other differences, such as different race and class experiences, different styles of expressing femininity or masculinity, or different modes of interacting in same-gender spaces. In any case, if someone's discomfort about a perceived difference leads you to resist thinking of someone as part of your gender "club," using the wrong pronoun can be a conscious or unconscious way to reinforce that separation.

Sometimes it's not so much about being in the same gender club, as about being in the same dating pool. A trans* woman I spoke with described how heterosexual cisgender men who find her attractive never seem to have any problem calling her "she," although they know she's trans*. On the other hand, heterosexual men who accidentally call her "he" are never those who find her attractive—or at least they never admit to it. Perhaps the men who easily call her the right pronouns use their attraction to her as evidence that she's "really" a woman (which would be an interesting kind of sexism!). Or maybe it's that men who don't want to think that they could be attracted to a trans* woman call her "he" as a sort of defense against finding her attractive—as a way to define her as outside the group of women they could possibly be attracted to.

Reflection: In-Groups
What does it mean for you to see someone as "like" you or "not like" you in terms of gender? What does it mean for you to see someone as "like" or "not like" the kind of people you could be attracted to? How might that get in the way of your respecting their genders?

Reflections: Exploring Interpersonal Factors
This works best if you have one specific person in mind, for whom you have particular difficulty using the right pronouns. Through reflective journaling or discussion with someone you trust, explore the following questions:

- How do you feel about this person? personally? professionally?
- Who else in your life does this person remind you of? How do you feel about those people?
- How has your relationship with this person been positive? How has it been negative?
- If you were to describe this person to a good friend on another continent (who would never meet them, so you wouldn't feel bad about gossiping), what would you say?
- Do you find the person attractive? If so, how do you see this as aligning, or not, with your sexual orientation?
- If relevant, say aloud to yourself, "[The person's name] is like me. [The person's name] is one of us [or 'one of the guys/girls/however you describe yourself and your gender peers]." Notice how you feel when you say it. Do you want this person in your in-group? Why or why not?
- In one relatively short sentence, describe your feelings about this person and then add "and at the same time I respect (his/her/their/etc.) gender and can demonstrate my respect in my language when I refer to (him/her/them/etc.)"—using the pronoun the person has asked you to use, of course! Write it down, and put it somewhere that you'll see it every day. Say it aloud whenever you see it, until it feels true and the pronouns become a habit.

WALLS HAVE EARS

Are there some situations in which you consistently use the right pronouns for a trans* friend, and other situations in which you tend to mess up? What does it depend on?

You might find that it depends on who else is in the room: the person you're talking about, other friends, colleagues, strangers, or no one. The difference is usually unconscious. In some cases, it may simply be that when the person you're talking about is not present it's easier to forget—especially if their pronoun change is recent. Even though that person can't hear you,

it is still important to get their pronoun right. Other people may take your language as a cue about what is acceptable. If you say the wrong pronoun and don't correct yourself aloud, they may assume that it is okay for them to use the wrong pronoun as well.

Sometimes, the unconscious difference in pronoun use in different situations might be serving to help you avoid some kind of discomfort. If your pronoun use tends to vary depending on who's listening, consider what discomfort you might be avoiding—even without intending to. For example, are you avoiding the discomfort of having to explain yourself to someone who might be less familiar with trans* issues than you are? Or the discomfort of worrying that you might be seen as sympathetic or close to the trans* community? Whatever it is, challenge yourself to make decisions with everyone's wellbeing in mind, rather than reacting instinctively to avoid discomfort.

Keep in mind that you can "out" someone, and potentially put them in danger, by using the wrong pronoun or *sometimes by using the right pronoun.* When someone has recently started using a new pronoun, it is a good practice to ask them who they've shared that information with already, and whether they want you to call them the new pronoun in all situations (thereby possibly outing them to some new people), or not. In some cases they may ask you to wait until they've had a chance to spread the word themself, or they may ask you to keep their transition confidential indefinitely.

Community Norms about Pronouns

In many trans*-friendly spaces, there is a community norm that we don't make assumptions about anyone's gender or pronoun preference. Instead we assume that gender identity cannot be observed or measured—the only way to know someone's gender identity is if they tell you. In these spaces it is usual to ask everyone to introduce themself to the group by sharing their name and pronoun, because we know that you can't tell by looking. It's also normal and acceptable to ask someone individually, "what pronouns do you want to be called?"

Some trans* people (and most cisgender people) want their pronouns to be obvious. They assume that by expressing their gender in an obviously feminine way, for example, they are sending a clear signal that people should call them she/her/hers pronouns. And it's true that more often than not, an ally can make a good guess at someone's pronouns based on their gender expression.

Nevertheless, assuming that everyone's gender will be obvious is problematic, because not everyone's is. A feminine person does not necessarily identify as a woman and want to be called she/her/hers. A masculine person does not necessarily identify as a man and want to be called he/him/his. An androgynous-looking person, like anyone else, may identify as a man, woman, both, neither, and/or something else, and some people don't particularly identify with any of these categories. And masculine, feminine, and androgynous (along with other gender expression categories) are culturally-specific, time-bound, basically made up categories that mean different things to different people. The only sure way to know someone's gender identity (which you rarely need to know) and pronoun (which you often do need to know) is to ask them.

When we assume that people's genders are necessarily so obvious that we can guess, rather than ask, we put a great burden on people whose gender and/or culture varies from the dominant expectation. Rather than making it everybody's responsibility to pay attention to how each person wants to be talked about, it becomes trans* people's responsibilities to present our genders convincingly. To be convincingly womanly, for example, means conforming to stereotyped and stylized versions of what it means to be a woman, which are unrealistic and restrictive to all women, trans* and cisgender alike. The practice of suspending assumptions and creating opportunities for people to describe their genders on their own terms—or to decline to describe them—resists sexism and trans* oppression and opens up the possibilities for everybody.

Tools: Community Norms

What are the norms about pronouns in your community? Have you ever heard anyone ask someone else what pronouns they want to be called? Have you ever shared pronouns as part of group introductions in a meeting or class? How sure are you of the pronoun preferences of the people you work or study with?

If you have never asked someone what pronouns they want to be called, try it. Ask someone in a one-on-one setting. Be prepared to explain where the question is coming from, since people unfamiliar with this practice may be really confused! TIP: Don't start by asking the one gender-nonconforming person in the group. It's good to notice if you are particularly *unsure* of one person's pronouns, but don't let that trick you into assuming that you are correct in your assumptions about everyone else.

Does your group already have a routine of starting with an introductory check-in? If so, try adding pronouns to that routine. Explain to the group or to a group leader that you've been reading and thinking about gender, and that this is one way some communities try to create a welcoming environment for trans* people. This can be awkward at first, until the group has a reliable shared understanding of the purpose of the exercise, but they'll get used to it. TIP: If you know of trans* or gender-nonconforming people in your group, check in with them *before* initiating a new group practice, so that you can think through potential unintended consequences and help make sure the shift will be positive for them.

Keep it Going!

Congratulations! If you've gotten this far you have done more thinking about gender and trans* experience than most cisgender people, and probably some trans* people. No reading or exercise can flip a magic switch to make gender or pronouns easy for you, or to undo all the counterproductive messages we've all been taught to believe about gender. But your honest reflection and practice will help you move in the world with integrity as a good friend and a reliable ally.

Remember that getting pronouns right is only one part of being a trans* ally. What else will you do? Will you continue to educate yourself and your community through reading, discussion, events or training? Will you focus on supporting individual trans* people you know? Or will you find ways to support trans* rights on a broader level, through joining the work of organizations like those listed below? However you choose to move forward with this work, I hope the tools you've learned here will prove helpful in approaching your work thoughtfully and well.

Resources

+ Audrey Lorde Project (NYC): http://alp.org/
+ Basic Rights Oregon: www.basicrights.org/
+ COLAGE resources for kids of trans* parents:
  http://www.colage.org/resources/kot/
+ FORGE (Madison, WI): http://forge-forward.org/
+ Gender Justice League (WA state): www.genderjusticeleague.org/
+ Global Action for Trans Equality: http://transactivists.org/
+ Massachusetts Transgender Political Coalition (MA):
  http://www.masstpc.org/
+ National Center for Transgender Equality: http://transequality.org/
+ National Gay and Lesbian Task Force:
  http://www.thetaskforce.org/issues/transgender
+ PFLAG trans* family resources: http://community.pflag.org/transgender
+ Sylvia Rivera Law Project (NYC): http://www.srlp.org/
+ TGEU (Europe): http://tgeu.org/
+ TGI Justice Project (CA): http://www.tgijp.org/
+ Transgender Law & Policy Institute: http://www.transgenderlaw.org/
+ Transgender Law Center (CA): http://www.transgenderlawcenter.org/
+ Trans People of Color Coalition: http://www.transpoc.org/
+ WPATH (World Professional Association of Transgender Health
  Professionals): http://www.wpath.org/

GLOSSARY

Language about trans* identities and experiences is constantly evolving, and different people may use these terms in different ways. A more extensive (and regularly updated) glossary is available at www.thinkagaintraining.com.

Gender and Sexual Orientation Concepts

BIOLOGICAL SEX AND SEX ASSIGNED AT BIRTH: "Sex" refers to one's body—the physiological and anatomical characteristics of maleness and femaleness with which a person is born or that develop with physical maturity. BIOLOGICAL SEX MARKERS include internal and external reproductive organs, chromosomes, hormone levels, and secondary sex characteristics such as facial hair and breasts. SEX ASSIGNED AT BIRTH is the sex category (almost always male or female) assigned to each of us on ID documents, beginning with the birth certificate.

GENDER EXPRESSION refers to appearance and behaviors that convey something about one's gender identity, or that others interpret as conveying something about one's gender identity, including clothing, mannerisms, communication patterns, etc.

GENDER IDENTITY refers to people's own understandings of themselves in terms of gendered categories like man and woman, boy and girl, transgender, genderqueer, and many others. Gender identity cannot be observed; the only way you can know someone's gender identity is if they tell you. Some people's gender identity is consistent for their whole lives; other people experience shifts in their gender identity over time.

PASSING means being seen as belonging unquestionably to a particular group, e.g. being seen as a woman or as a man. Often, it refers to a trans* person being seen as the gender they are; occasionally it refers to being seen as the gender as which one wants to be seen at the moment, for safety or other reasons. Some people use "passing" specifically to mean being seen as cisgender (e.g. a trans* woman who is assumed by others to be a cisgender woman is "passing"), while for others it is not that specific. Passing is a very complex and problematic concept, not only with regard to trans* issues but also in terms of race, class, and other systems of categorization and power. Useful thoughts on some of the problems with "passing" can be found in Julia Serano's book *Whipping Girl* (Chapter 8).

SEXUAL ORIENTATION describes an individual's patterns of romantic and/or sexual attraction, in terms of gender. For example someone may be attracted to people of the same gender as themself, to people of a particular other gender, or to people of all genders. Sexual orientation is not the same as gender expression or gender identity. People of any gender may have any sexual orientation.

TRANSITION can refer to any of the medical, social, legal, spiritual and personal processes that a trans* person may go through in order to live their life in a way that works for their gender.

Identity Categories

CISGENDER (adj.): Non-trans*. From a Latin prefix meaning "on the same side," as opposed to trans- which means "across." Describes people whose gender identity matches what is expected of them in their culture based on their sex assigned at birth—e.g. people assigned male at birth who identify as men and people assigned female at birth who identify as women.

CROSS DRESSER (n.): A person who enjoys dressing in clothes typically associated with the other of the two socially sanctioned genders. Most cross dressers are heterosexual men who enjoy wearing women's clothes occasionally.

DRAG KINGS AND DRAG QUEENS (n.): Drag is the practice of dressing and acting in an exaggerated masculine or feminine way, usually playfully and for theatrical performance. DRAG QUEENS are usually men whose performances highlight femininity; DRAG KINGS are usually women whose performances highlight masculinity. People with nonbinary gender identities can also do drag; e.g. a genderqueer person whose drag performance highlights masculinity can be a drag king.

GENDERQUEER (adj.): One of many identity labels used by trans* people whose gender identity does not fit into either of the two culturally accepted gender categories (men and women). Genderqueer means different things to different people, and genderqueer people look, act and describe themselves in a wide variety of ways. However, genderqueer is not an umbrella term; you should only refer to someone as genderqueer if you know that they want to be described that way.

INTERSEX (adj.): Describes someone whose anatomy or physiology is not easily categorized as simply male or female. This may be noticed at birth, or may not be apparent until puberty. Some intersex people are also trans*, and many others are not. For more information regarding intersexuality, see http://www.accordalliance.org

QUEER (adj.): An umbrella term describing a wide range of people who do not conform to heterosexual and/or gender norms; a reclaimed derogatory slur taken as a political term to unite people who are marginalized because of their nonconformance to dominant gender identities and/or heterosexuality. Sometimes used as a shortcut for LGBT. Other times used to distinguish politically queer people from more mainstream LGBT people. *Because of its origin as a derogatory slur, this term should be used thoughtfully. If you're not queer, or for public communications, LGBT is often more appropriate.*

TRANS* (adj.): Anyone whose GENDER IDENTITY and/or GENDER EXPRESSION differs significantly from what is expected of them in their culture based on their SEX ASSIGNED AT BIRTH. This broad category includes transgender, transsexual and genderqueer people, cross dressers, drag queens and kings, masculine women and feminine men, and more. The asterisk is there to remind us that trans* includes *everyone* who could be described this way, not only a particular subset of trans* people. We use the term so broadly because it enables us to talk about issues facing the whole range of trans* people—but it's important to remember that not everyone who could be described as trans* in this definition self-identifies as a trans* person.

TRANS (adj.): Can be used as broadly as trans*, or can be short for transgender as defined below.

TRANSGENDER (adj.): Can be used as broadly as trans*, but more often refers specifically to trans* people who have an experience of transitioning (socially, legally and/or medically) from living as one gender to living as another gender. TIP: Transgender should almost always be used as an adjective. As a noun (e.g. "she's a transgender") it sounds disrespectful to many people, and as a past-tense verb ("transgendered") it does not make any sense.

TRANSSEXUAL (adj.): Usually, a person who experiences an intense, persistent, and long-term feeling that their body and assigned sex are at odds with their gender identity. Such individuals often (but not always) desire to change their bodies to bring then into alignment with their gender identities. This term originated as a medical diagnosis, and many people do not identify with it for that reason.

TRANS MAN (or transgender man, or transsexual man) (n.): An FTM trans* person. Someone assigned female at birth who now identifies and lives as a man. FTM/ F2M/ FTM (adj.): Female-to-Male, or Female-toward-Male, trans* person.

TRANS WOMAN (or transgender woman, or transsexual woman) (n.): An MTF trans person. Someone assigned male at birth who now identifies and lives as a woman. MTF/ M2F/ MTF (adj.): Male-to-Female, or Male-toward-Female, trans* person.

ABOUT THINK AGAIN TRAINING & CONSULTATION

Think Again provides educational design and facilitation services including workshops, in-depth training retreats, and training of trainers, as well as organizational assessments and policy consultation. We help schools, workplaces and communities to

- develop *critical consciousness* about issues of oppression and social justice
- gain *skills* to enact justice in our work and in our lives
- engage in informed and compassionate *dialogue across differences*
- work together *effectively and joyfully*

Some areas of special focus include Gender & Trans* Inclusion, and Class, Classism & Cross-Class Communication. Find out more at www.thinkagaintraining.com, or contact us at davey@ thinkagaintraining.com to inquire about scheduling a training.

This book, and the workshops that go with it, are an ongoing project that benefits from community input and feedback. If you have a story about how this booklet has been helpful to you, or if you have feedback about how you'd like it to be different, please get in touch: davey@thinkagaintraining.com.

ABOUT THE AUTHOR:
Davey Shlasko is the founder of Think Again Training, and an educator, consultant and writer, whose passion is facilitating group learning about & in the context of social justice movements. Davey works in classroom, workplace and community settings, combining expressive arts, introspective exploration, academic theory and hands-on skills-building to help groups deepen understanding and practice of social justice principles. Davey has been writing and teaching about trans* issues since 2000, and earned an M.Ed. in Social Justice Education from the University of Massachusetts, Amherst.

ABOUT THE ILLUSTRATOR:
Kai Hofius is a poet, illustrator, and full stack web developer-in-training. You can find more of their work at www.kaihofi.us

CPSIA information can be obtained
at www.ICGtesting.com
Printed in the USA
LVOW02s1702290916

506490LV00035B/114/P

9 780990 636908